How to
BELIEVE GOD
for a house

GLORIA COPELAND & PASTOR GEORGE PEARSONS

For more information about Kenneth Copeland Ministries, visit kcm.org or call 1-800-600-7395 (U.S. only) or +1-817-852-6000.

ISBN 978-1-57562-636-9
#30-0828

Unless otherwise noted, all scripture is from the *King James Version* of the Bible.

*t*Scripture quotations marked *The Amplified Bible* or AMP are from *The Amplified Bible, Old Testament* © 1965, 1987 by the Zondervan Corporation. *The Amplified New Testament* © 1958, 1987 by The Lockman Foundation. Used by permission.

Scripture quotations marked *New International Version* or NIV are from *The Holy Bible, New International Version* © 1973, 1978, 1984, 2011 by Biblica Inc. Used by permission. All rights reserved worldwide.

Scripture quotations marked NIV-84 are from *The Holy Bible, New International Version* © 1973, 1978, 1984, by Biblica Inc. Used by permission. All rights reserved worldwide.

Scripture quotations marked NLT are from the *Holy Bible, New Living Translation* © 1996, 2004, 2007 by Tyndale Charitable Trust. Used by permission of Tyndale House Publishers.

Scripture quotations marked *The Message* or MSG are from *The Message* © 1993, 1994, 1995, 1996, 2000, 2001, 2002. Used by permission of NavPress Publishing Group.

Scripture quotations marked DRB are from the *1899 Douay-Rheims Bible*, public domain.

Scripture quotations marked YLT are from *Young's Literal Translation*, Robert Young, 1898, public domain.

Scripture quotations marked HCSB are from the *Holman Christian Standard Bible*, © 1999, 2000, 2003, 2009 by Holman Bible Publishers. Used by permission.

Scripture quotations marked DARBY are from the *Darby Translation*, John Nelson Darby, 1890, public domain.

Day #2 quotes from Gloria Copeland, *God's Will Is Prosperity* (Fort Worth, Kenneth Copeland Publications, 1978), pages 50-51.

Day #9 quote from Kenneth Copeland, Kenneth and Gloria Copeland, *From Faith to Faith—A Daily Guide to Victory* (Fort Worth: Kenneth Copeland Publications, 1992), November 13 devotion.

Excerpts from Gloria Copeland, *God's Will Is Prosperity* (Fort Worth, Kenneth Copeland Publications, 1978), Chapter 3, "Divine Prosperity."

"How to Believe God for a House" article by George Pearsons, published in the October 2013 edition of the *Believer's Voice of Victory* magazine, © 2013 Eagle Mountain International Church Inc. aka Kenneth Copeland Ministries.

Faith Scriptures for Your New Home by Gloria Copeland, © 2004 Eagle Mountain International Church Inc. aka Kenneth Copeland Ministries.

HOW TO BELIEVE GOD
for a house

Table of Contents

God's Will for Your House

Day #1

A.   1 John 5:14-15—Where Faith for a House Begins
   1.   AMP: "And this is the confidence (the assurance, the privilege of boldness) which we have in Him: [we are sure] that if we ask anything (make any request) according to His will (in agreement with His own plan), He listens to and hears us. And if (since) we [positively] know that He listens to us in whatever we ask, we also know [with settled and absolute knowledge] that we have [granted us as our present possessions] the requests made of Him."
   2.   Faith stops at the question mark.
   3.   Faith for a house begins where the will of God is known.
   4.   God's Word is God's perfect will.
   5.   You must know from God's Word that it is His will for you to live in a beautiful, debt-free house.

B.   Genesis 2:8—The Garden of Eden
   1.   AMP: "And the Lord God planted a garden toward the east, in Eden [delight]; and there He put the man whom He had formed (framed, constituted)."
   2.   *Eden* (HEB) = The region of Adam's home; House of Pleasure; luxury
   3.   The Garden of Eden was God's original intent for our earthly homes.
   4.   Because of THE BLESSING, our surroundings should be like the Garden of Eden.
   5.   Our homes should be a refuge; places that minister the life of God.

C.   Isaiah 32:18—Your Peaceful Habitation
   1.   *Habitation* (HEB) = Home, residence, dwelling, pleasant place
   2.   NIV: "My people will live in peaceful dwelling places, in secure homes, in undisturbed places of rest."
   3.   MSG: "My people will live in a peaceful neighborhood—in safe houses, in quiet gardens."
   4.   DRB: "My people shall sit in the beauty of peace, and in the tabernacles of confidence, and in wealthy rest."
   5.   NLT: "My people will live in safety, quietly at home. They will be at rest."

HOW TO BELIEVE GOD
for a house

_____
_____
_____
_____
_____
_____
_____
_____
_____
_____
_____
_____
_____
_____
_____
_____
_____
_____
_____
_____
_____
_____
_____

Through wisdom is an house builded; and by understanding it is established: And by knowledge shall the chambers be filled with all precious and pleasant riches.

PROVERBS 24:3-4

Through wisdom is an house builded; and by understanding it is established: And by knowledge shall the chambers be filled with all precious and pleasant riches.

PROVERBS 24:3-4

How to Believe God for a house

A Debt-Free Stand of Faith

Day #2

A. **Romans 13:8 (AMP)—Keep Out of Debt**
   1. In 1967, Kenneth and Gloria determined that whatever they saw in God's Word, they would do.
   2. "If faith won't get it, we won't have it. If the Word won't get it, we don't need it."
   3. Then they found Romans 13:8 (AMP) that says, "Keep out of debt and owe no man anything, except to love one another."
   4. They committed to live debt free.
   5. From God's Will Is Prosperity by Gloria Copeland
      a. "The first thing I began to believe God for was a home."
      b. "But what about Romans 13:8? It says that we are to owe no man anything but to love Him. How can you believe God for enough money to buy a home?
      c. "This is one area most people think is impossible."
      d. "Many have made the statement, 'Surely you don't have to believe for a home without borrowing money!'"

B. **2 Corinthians 9:8 (AMP)—"I hung my faith on that scripture."**
   1. "Satan would come to me with thoughts of doubt and say, 'There is no way that you can buy a house without going into debt.' When he would do that, I would trust in and continually confess 2 Corinthians 9:8 (AMP). It gave me the comfort and strength I needed to stand in faith."
   2. "And God is able to make all grace (every favor and earthly blessing) come to you in abundance, so that you may always and under all circumstances and whatever the need be self-sufficient [possessing enough to require no aid or support and furnished in abundance for every good work and charitable donation]."
   3. "I hung my faith on that scripture."
   4. "Believing God was the only way I could have my home."
   5. "The Word says that He is able to get it to you."

C. **James 1:5-8—Stay Single-Minded on the Word**

    1.   "When I believe God for something, I don't waver."

    2.   "I have made a quality decision that the Word is true."

    3.   "I have built into myself a reliance on God's Word."

    4.   "I believe His Word more than I believe what I can see or feel."

        a. "You've got to dump your fear to make your stand." —Gloria Copeland (statement made during the recording of this series)

    5.   "As I have heard Kenneth Hagin say, 'If you are determined to stand forever, it won't take very long.'"

        a. "That's the way I am when I am believing God for something."

        b. "I could stand forever if necessary."

"The Word says that He is able to get it to you. Don't look to natural sources. Don't look to your job. When you are believing God, you have to look to His Word. Keep your eye single on the Word. You have to realize and know that He can and will work in your behalf. God is a real operator! He is able to get things done."

—Gloria Copeland, God's Will Is Prosperity

How to Believe God
for a house

_____
_____
_____
_____
_____
_____
_____
_____
_____
_____
_____
_____
_____
_____
_____
_____
_____
_____
_____
_____
_____

Through wisdom is an house builded; and by understanding it is established: And by knowledge shall the chambers be filled with all precious and pleasant riches.

PROVERBS 24:3-4

Through wisdom is an house builded; and by understanding it is established: And by knowledge shall the chambers be filled with all precious and pleasant riches.

PROVERBS 24:3-4

Three Revelations—Part 1

Day #3

A. **Mark 11:24—Faith Begins With Believing**
1. "We began believing God for the perfect home when we lived in Tulsa, Oklahoma, in 1968."
2. "At the same time, there was a lady in Fort Worth, Texas, who started building her home."
3. "It was several years before I saw that home, but the floor plan was exactly what we needed to meet our needs as a family. It was perfect for us."
4. "She began to build it at the very time we began to believe for it."
5. "God started to work immediately."
   a. After moving back to Fort Worth, Kenneth and Gloria looked at the house.
   b. The owners tried to sell it, even give it away—but it was given back.
   c. "They couldn't even give it away! That was our home!"

B. **2 Corinthians 4:13—Speak What You Believe**
1. "We leased the house for one year. We agreed to pay cash for it at the end of that year."
2. "We lived well. But as far as having that much money in cash, we just didn't have it. In the natural there was no reason to expect to have it, but in the spirit we knew our God was able."
   a. "We could have borrowed the money years sooner, but we refused to compromise on our decision."
   b. "Whenever there is a choice between the world's way and the Word's way, we always go with the Word."
3. "When we moved in, the house was in need of repair. It needed to be completely remodeled, so I was faced with a decision."
   a. "I had enough money to start the remodeling."
   b. "This is not our house legally. It would be unwise to put thousands of dollars into a house that doesn't even belong to us."
4. "As an act of faith, I went to work."
5. "When Satan would say, 'That sure is a lot of money for you to lose,' I would answer, 'No, in the Name of Jesus, this is my house and it will be paid for in July. We will pay cash for it and I believe I have the money in the Name of Jesus!'"

C. Gloria Copeland's Three Revelations Came While Believing for the Money
1. The Revelation of Divine Prosperity
2. The Revelation of Peace and Prosperity
3. The Revelation of Dominion and Authority

D. Galatians 3:13-14—The Revelation of Divine Prosperity
1. "Our commitment years before to stay out of debt made the difference."
2. "If we had not committed to God's Word then, we would not know what we know today about God's system of finance."
3. "One day as I was standing in my house, looking out the window and thinking about these things, God gave me what I would call a revelation of divine prosperity."
    a. "Divine prosperity works exactly the same way as divine healing."
    b. "We would allow symptoms of lack to come on us and stay there. We were willing to tolerate them."
    c. "I realized that Jesus bore the curse of poverty at the same time He bore the curse of sickness."
4. "You can believe for divine prosperity just as you believe for divine health. Both blessings already belong to you. You should refuse lack just as quickly as you refuse sickness."
5. "If you make up your mind—make a quality decision—that you are not willing to live in lack, but that you are willing to live in divine prosperity and abundance, Satan cannot stop the flow of God's financial blessings."
    a. Declare: "I am not willing to live in lack."
    b. Confess: "I am living in divine prosperity!"

How to Believe God
for a house

_____

_____

_____

_____

_____

_____

_____

_____

_____

_____

_____

_____

_____

_____

_____

_____

_____

_____

_____

_____

_____

_____

_____

_____

_____

Through wisdom is an house builded; and by understanding it is established: And by knowledge shall the chambers be filled with all precious and pleasant riches.

PROVERBS 24:3-4

Through wisdom is an house builded; and by understanding it is established: And by knowledge shall the chambers be filled with all precious and pleasant riches.

Three Revelations—Part 2

Day #4

A. Galatians 3:13-14—The Revelation of Divine Prosperity
1. Kenneth and Gloria were leasing a house, believing God to buy it at the end of a year.
2. The Lord gave Gloria three revelations of how to believe God for her house.
3. The first was a revelation of divine prosperity.
4. The Lord showed her that she was to stand in faith for her prosperity in the same way that she would stand in faith for her healing.
   a. Just as Jesus had borne her sicknesses and diseases, He had paid for her to be free from poverty and lack.
   b. "We need to see prosperity in the same light that we see healing and health."
5. "You begin to walk in divine prosperity with a decision to no longer allow Satan to put symptoms of lack on you."

B. Isaiah 53:5, 48:17-18—The Revelation of Peace and Prosperity
1. Isaiah 53:5: "The chastisement of our peace was upon him."
2. Isaiah 48:17-18 (AMP): "Thus says the Lord, your Redeemer, the Holy One of Israel: I am the Lord your God, Who teaches you to profit, Who leads you in the way that you should go. Oh, that you had hearkened to My commandments! Then your peace and prosperity would have been like a flowing river, and your righteousness [the holiness and purity of the nation] like the [abundant] waves of the sea."
3. Genesis 15:1 (AMP): "Peace and well-being include a prosperous life. God told Abram, 'Fear not, Abram, I am your Shield, your abundant compensation, and your reward shall be exceedingly great.'"
   a. "Abundant compensation is far-reaching."
   b. "Abundant compensation means everything."
   c. "It enveloped Abraham in a blanket of well-being."
4. "Peace and prosperity go hand in hand. Your prosperity has already been provided for you. Prosperity is yours. Rest in that."
5. *Peace* (HEB) = Nothing missing, nothing broken
6. "Peace is everything that makes for man's highest good." —Gloria Copeland

C. Genesis 1:26-28—The Revelation of Dominion and Authority

1. Divine prosperity and abundance belong to you now.
2. We, as born-again believers, have the same authority over the earth that Adam had in the Garden of Eden.
3. Verse 28 (AMP): "And God blessed them and said to them, Be fruitful, multiply, and fill the earth, and subdue it [using all its vast resources...]."
4. "While we were standing in faith for the money to pay for our house, the Lord reminded me of this scripture and revealed to me that every material thing here came from the earth's vast resources. Every piece of lumber, brick, glass, concrete, mortar—there was nothing in the makeup of our house that had not come from the earth's resources."
   a. "I wasn't taking authority over something that belonged to someone else. That house was up for sale."
   b. "The people had relinquished their authority when they put it on the market."
   c. "I had the right to take authority over it and receive it as mine in the Name of Jesus."
5. "I began to see that I already had authority over that house and authority over the money I needed to purchase it. I said, 'In the Name of Jesus, I take authority over the money I need. I command you to come to me. I take my place and I take dominion over that which I need. I command it to come in Jesus' Name. Ministering spirits, you go and cause it to come.'"

How to Believe God
for a house

_____

_____

_____

_____

_____

_____

_____

_____

_____

_____

_____

_____

_____

_____

_____

_____

_____

_____

_____

_____

_____

Through wisdom is an house builded; and by understanding it is established: And by knowledge shall the chambers be filled with all precious and pleasant riches.

PROVERBS 24:3-4

Through wisdom is an house builded; and by understanding it is established: And by knowledge shall the chambers be filled with all precious and pleasant riches.

PROVERBS 24:3-4

How Far Will You Go on God's Word?

Day #5

A. **Ephesians 6:13-14—The Stand of Faith**
1. "It was six years from the time we started believing God for the perfect home until we moved into our home."
2. "At the end of the year's lease, we paid cash for our 'faith house.'"
3. "I am still not sure how, except by faith in God's Word."
4. "Had we borrowed the money, we would still have 35 years to pay!"
5. "Thank God, borrowed money is not our source—HE IS!"

B. **This Must Become a Revelation to You**
1. "You cannot receive these things just because I tell you about them."
2. "They must become real to you."
3. "You have to take the scriptures on prosperity and meditate on them until they become a reality in your heart, until you know that prosperity belongs to you."
4. Once you have a revelation of divine prosperity, peace and prosperity, and dominion and authority in your spirit, you won't allow Satan to take it from you.
5. "The Word of God is the source of your prosperity."

C. **Excerpt From a Partner Letter by Kenneth Copeland**
1. "Ask yourself: 'Just how far will I go on the Word?'"
2. "When God told Israel that He would make them plenteous in goods and they would lend to many nations and borrow from none, He meant He would supply them better than if they went to another nation."
3. "When Gloria and I decided to owe no man anything, we made that decision to glorify God and please God by walking by faith. We started by making the quality decision to borrow no more and released our faith to pay all the debts we owed. We were faced with believing for our everyday supply. We learned to believe for the small things first."
4. "As God taught us to prosper, the day came when we knew we were ready to have a home. We were faced with the same question I told you to ask yourself. How far will we go on the Word? We made the decision then if we ever had a choice we would use our faith instead of some other source."
5. "We were in a good enough financial position to have borrowed the money and lived in a better house than the one we were living in all of those eight years. Believe me, the faith way was better. We have the perfect home. It is not just a nice home…. The Word is strong enough in any situation."

HOW TO BELIEVE GOD
for a house

_____

_____

_____

_____

_____

_____

_____

_____

_____

_____

_____

_____

_____

_____

_____

_____

_____

_____

_____

_____

_____

_____

_____

Through wisdom is an house builded; and by understanding it is established: And by knowledge shall the chambers be filled with all precious and pleasant riches.

PROVERBS 24:3-4

Through wisdom is an house builded; and by understanding it is established: And by knowledge shall the chambers be filled with all precious and pleasant riches.

PROVERBS 24:3-4

How to Believe God
for a house

21 House Scriptures—Part 1

Day #6

1. Proverbs 24:3-4 (AMP): "Through skillful and godly Wisdom is a house (a life, a home, a family) built, and by understanding it is established [on a sound and good foundation], and by knowledge shall its chambers [of every area] be filled with all precious and pleasant riches."
   a. MSG: "It takes wisdom to build a house, and understanding to see it on a firm foundation."
   b. HCSB: "A house is built by wisdom."

2. Proverbs 9:1 (AMP): "Wisdom has built her house."

3. Proverbs 14:1 (AMP): "Every wise woman builds her house, but the foolish one tears it down with her own hands."
   a. DARBY: "The wisdom of women buildeth their house."
   b. Ruth 4:11: "Rachel and Leah…did build the house of Israel."

4. Isaiah 65:21: "They shall build homes and inhabit them; and they shall plant vineyards, and eat the fruit of them."

5. Proverbs 24:27 (AMP): "[Put first things first.] Prepare your work outside and get it ready for yourself in the field; and afterward build your house and establish a home."

6. Jeremiah 29:5 (AMP): "Build yourselves houses and dwell in them; plant gardens and eat the fruit of them."

7. Psalm 107:7 (AMP): "He led them forth by the straight and right way, that they might go to a city where they could establish their homes."
   a. MSG: "He put your feet on a wonderful road that took you straight to a good place to live."

House Scriptures
Is 32:17-18 New
Ps 18:19 large place
66:12

Ps 31:18-19
1 Cor 2:7-10 =
Prepared!
2 Sam 7:10 KJNIV
"place of their own"

Prov 24:3-4, 27 Amp timing. Ps 127:1
v.12 fine homes ALT

Deut 6:10-11   8:1-10, 18- (fountains)

~~Ps. 68:6   Luke 4:18~~   Add: to list

Ps 107:7-9 Amp   Prov 8:21

Ps 112:1-5

Ps 118: 5,23   large place

Prov 9:1   12:7   15:6 Amp

       10:22   22:4

Is 32:17-18 Amp   Timing =
                        Prov 24:27

Jer 29: 4-~~10~~   28

       31:12-14

Ps 107:29, 29-32, 35-38, 41-43 Amp

Ps 66:12

Ps 68: 3-6, 10 19 Amp (Luke 4:18)

Amos 9:13-15   landscape
                        Ps 78:55 T995
Acts 17:26   Ps 16:5-6 Ps 127:1

How to Believe God for a house

_____

_____

_____

_____

_____

_____

_____

_____

_____

_____

_____

_____

_____

_____

_____

_____

_____

_____

_____

_____

Through wisdom is an house builded; and by understanding it is established: And by knowledge shall the chambers be filled with all precious and pleasant riches.

PROVERBS 24:3-4

Through wisdom is an house builded; and by understanding it is established: And by knowledge shall the chambers be filled with all precious and pleasant riches.

21 House Scriptures—Part 2

Day #7

8.   Psalm 18:19 (AMP): "He brought me forth also into a large place; He was delivering me because He was pleased with me and delighted in me."
     a.   HEB—A roomy place with wide expanses
     b.   NIV—A spacious place

9.   Psalm 66:12: "Thou hast caused men to ride over our heads; we went through fire and through water: but thou broughtest us out into a wealthy place."
     a.   NIV—A place of abundance
     b.   YLT—A watered place

10. 2 Samuel 7:10: "Moreover I will appoint a place for my people Israel, and will plant them, that they may dwell in a place of their own, and move no more; neither shall the children of wickedness afflict them any more, as beforetime."
     a.   NIV—A home of their own

11. John 14:2: "In my Father's house are many mansions: if it were not so, I would have told you. I go to prepare a place for you."

12. Proverbs 12:7 (AMP): "The wicked are overthrown and are not, but the house of the [uncompromisingly] righteous shall stand."
     a.   NIV—Stands firm
     b.   MSG: "The homes of good people hold together."

13. Isaiah 32:18 (MSG): "My people will live in a peaceful neighborhood—in safe houses, in quiet gardens."

14. Psalm 78:55 (NIV): "He drove out nations before them and allotted their lands to them as an inheritance; he settled the tribes of Israel in their homes."

How to Believe God
for a house

_____
_____
_____
_____
_____
_____
_____
_____
_____
_____
_____
_____
_____
_____
_____
_____
_____
_____
_____
_____
_____
_____

Through wisdom is an house builded; and by understanding it is established: And by knowledge shall the chambers be filled with all precious and pleasant riches.

PROVERBS 24:3-4

Through wisdom is an house builded; and by understanding it is established: And by knowledge shall the chambers be filled with all precious and pleasant riches.

PROVERBS 24:3-4

21 House Scriptures—Part 3

Day #8

15. Proverbs 3:33 (NIV): "The Lord's curse is on the house of the wicked, but he blesses the home of the righteous."
    a. DRB: "The habitations of the just shall be blessed."

16. Acts 17:26 (AMP): "And He made from one [common origin, one source, one blood] all nations of men to settle on the face of the earth, having definitely determined [their] allotted periods of time and the fixed boundaries of their habitation (their settlements, lands, and abodes)."
    a. NIV-84: "He determined the times set for them and the exact places where they should live."

17. Psalm 16:5-6 (NLT): "Lord, you alone are my inheritance, my cup of blessing. You guard all that is mine. The land you have given me is a pleasant land. What a wonderful inheritance!"
    a. MSG: "My choice is you, God, first and only. And now I find I'm your choice! You set me up with a house and yard. And then you made me your heir!"

18. Proverbs 14:11 (NLT): "The house of the wicked will be destroyed, but the tent of the godly will flourish."

19. Psalm 68:6 (AMP): "God places the solitary in families and gives the desolate a home in which to dwell; He leads the prisoners out to prosperity; but the rebellious dwell in a parched land."

20. Psalm 127:1 (NIV-84): "Unless the Lord builds the house, its builders labor in vain. Unless the Lord watches over the city, the watchmen stand guard in vain."

21. Hebrews 11:10 (NIV): "For he was looking forward to the city with foundations, whose architect and builder is God."

Bonus Scriptures:

2 Samuel 7:27 (NIV): "Lord Almighty, God of Israel, you have revealed this to your servant, saying, 'I will build a house for you.'"

1 Chronicles 28:19 (MSG): "Here are the blueprints for the whole project as God gave me to understand it."

HOW TO BELIEVE GOD
for a house

_____
_____
_____
_____
_____
_____
_____
_____
_____
_____
_____
_____
_____
_____
_____
_____
_____
_____
_____
_____
_____
_____
_____
_____
_____

Through wisdom is an house builded; and by understanding it is established: And by knowledge shall the chambers be filled with all precious and pleasant riches.

PROVERBS 24:3-4

Through wisdom is an house builded; and by understanding it is established: And by knowledge shall the chambers be filled with all precious and pleasant riches.

PROVERBS 24:3-4

The Lord Will Furnish Your Home

Day #9

A. **Psalm 112:1, 3:** "Praise ye the Lord. Blessed is the man that feareth the Lord, that delighteth greatly in his commandments. Wealth and riches shall be in his house: and his righteousness endureth for ever."

"I'll never forget the time Gloria discovered that scripture. We didn't have any money at the time, and the walls in our house were as bare as they could be. But she was ready to decorate. So she took that promise, 'Wealth and riches shall be in his house' and laid claim to it by faith.

"Suddenly, everywhere we went, somebody was giving us a painting or some other little treasure for our house.

"Unfortunately, most believers aren't as quick to believe God for that kind of thing as Gloria was. Some even claim God doesn't promise us New Testament believers physical prosperity—just spiritual. But the truth is, you can't separate the two. That's why Jesus says if you'll seek first the kingdom of God and His righteousness, then all these (material) things will be added to you. He knows the spiritual realm and the material realm are connected.

"Don't let anyone talk you out of God's promises of prosperity. You don't have to choose between financial and spiritual prosperity. Both belong to you. Lay claim to them by faith. As a born-again child of God, dare to reach out and receive the riches that belong to you!"

—Kenneth Copeland, From Faith to Faith

B. **Home-Furnishing Scriptures**
    1. Deuteronomy 6:10-11 (AMP): "When the Lord your God brings you into the land which He swore to your fathers, to Abraham, Isaac, and Jacob, to give you, with great and goodly cities which you did not build, and houses full of all good things which you did not fill, and cisterns hewn out which you did not hew, and vineyards and olive trees which you did not plant."

2. Psalm 112:3 (MSG): "Their houses brim with wealth and a generosity that never runs dry."
3. Psalm 122:7 (AMP): "May peace be within your walls and prosperity within your palaces!"
4. Proverbs 15:6 (AMP): "In the house of the [uncompromisingly] righteous is great [priceless] treasure."
   a. NIV-84: "The house of the righteous contains great treasure."
5. Proverbs 24:3-4 (AMP): "Through skillful and godly Wisdom is a house (a life, a home, a family) built, and by understanding it is established [on a sound and good foundation], and by knowledge shall its chambers [of every area] be filled with all precious and pleasant riches."
   a. Verse 4 (NLT): "Through knowledge its rooms are filled with all sorts of precious riches and valuables."
   b. NIV: "Through knowledge its rooms are filled with rare and beautiful treasures."
   c. MSG: "It takes knowledge to furnish its rooms with fine furniture and beautiful drapes."
6. 1 Kings 6:38 (AMP): "In the eleventh year, in Bul, the eighth month, the house was finished throughout according to all its specifications. So he was seven years in building it."
7. Isaiah 61:4 (NIV): "They will rebuild the ancient ruins and restore the places long devastated; they will renew the ruined cities that have been devastated for generations." (A scripture for renovating a house.)
8. Isaiah 65:22 (MSG): "No more building a house that some outsider takes over. No more planting fields that some enemy confiscates." (A scripture for foreclosure.)

C. Confession of Home Furnishings
Father, in the Name of Jesus,
I thank You that You provide all things richly to enjoy.
That includes the furnishing of my home.
According to Your Word, I believe I receive:
　　Wealth and riches in my home.
　　My house brimming with wealth.
　　Houses full of all good things which I did not fill.
　　Peace within my walls and prosperity within my palaces.
　　Great and priceless treasure.
　　The chambers of every area filled with all precious
　　and pleasant riches and rare and beautiful treasures.
In the same way You furnished the Temple,
thank You for furnishing my home!

How to Believe God
for a house

_____
_____
_____
_____
_____
_____
_____
_____
_____
_____
_____
_____
_____
_____
_____
_____
_____
_____
_____
_____
_____

Through wisdom is an house builded; and by understanding it is established: And by knowledge shall the chambers be filled with all precious and pleasant riches.

PROVERBS 24:3-4

_____
_____
_____
_____
_____
_____
_____
_____
_____
_____
_____
_____
_____
_____
_____
_____
_____
_____
_____
_____
_____
_____
_____
_____
_____
_____
_____
_____
_____
_____

Through wisdom is an house builded; and by understanding it is established: And by knowledge shall the chambers be filled with all precious and pleasant riches.

PROVERBS 24:3-4

Stand Your Ground

Day #10

A. Galatians 6:9 (AMP): "And let us not lose heart and grow weary and faint in acting nobly and doing right, for in due time and at the appointed season we shall reap, if we do not loosen and relax our courage and faint."

1. You made the quality decision to believe God for a house.
2. You gathered your scriptures and declared them every day.
3. Time went by and there didn't seem to be much change.
4. You got discouraged and your faith began to wane.
5. A word of encouragement: STAND YOUR GROUND AND DON'T GIVE UP—NO MATTER HOW LONG IT TAKES TO BELIEVE GOD FOR YOUR HOUSE.

B. Hebrews 6:12: "That ye be not slothful, but followers of them who through faith and patience inherit the promises."

1. Patience is not passively hunkering down until the storm passes over, being satisfied with whatever happens.
2. Patience is a force that undergirds your faith that stands firm until the desired result is achieved.
    a. Patience stays in one spot and does not move.
    b. It does not bend or break but remains constant and unwavering.
    c. Faith takes whatever you need, and patience keeps it.
3. James 1:2-4 "My brethren, count it all joy when ye fall into divers temptations; knowing this, that the trying of your faith worketh patience. But let patience have her perfect work, that ye may be perfect and entire, wanting nothing."
    a. Verse 4 (AMP): "But let endurance and steadfastness and patience have full play and do a thorough work, so that you may be [people] perfectly and fully developed [with no defects], lacking in nothing."
    b. Verses 3-4 (NLT): "For you know that when your faith is tested, your endurance has a chance to grow. So let it grow, for when your endurance is fully developed, you will be perfect and complete, needing nothing."
4. Time can be an enemy or an opportunity.
    a. An enemy that causes you to become discouraged and quit.
    b. An opportunity to keep building your faith, watching it grow as you relentlessly refuse to give up.

5. The end result of standing: You will be fully developed in your faith, lacking nothing.

C. Hebrews 10:35-36 (AMP): "Do not, therefore, fling away your fearless confidence, for it carries a great and glorious compensation of reward. For you have need of steadfast patience and endurance, so that you may perform and fully accomplish the will of God, and thus receive and carry away [and enjoy to the full] what is promised."

1. After Terri and I paid for our house, it took us four years to move in.
2. There were times when we got discouraged. But we kept believing, stood our ground and refused to give up and quit.
3. We are thankful for the decision to pay for and renovate the house debt free.
4. We averted a 30-year mortgage, thousands of dollars in interest and did not bow our knee to a lender.
5. "I speak to my house in the Name of Jesus and command it to come to me! No matter how long it takes, I am standing my ground, walking by faith, holding fast to the Word and refusing to fling it away, throw in the towel and quit. I am strong in The Lord and in the power of His might. I believe I receive my debt-free house NOW!!"

How to Believe God
for a house

_____

_____

_____

_____

_____

_____

_____

_____

_____

_____

_____

_____

_____

_____

_____

_____

_____

_____

_____

_____

_____

Through wisdom is an house builded; and by understanding it is established: And by knowledge shall the chambers be filled with all precious and pleasant riches.

PROVERBS 24:3-4

Through wisdom is an house builded; and by understanding it is established: And by knowledge shall the chambers be filled with all precious and pleasant riches.

PROVERBS 24:3-4

40

HOW TO BELIEVE GOD FOR A HOUSE:
Our Personal Journey
Bonus Teaching with Pastors George and Terri Pearsons

"Every wise woman buildeth her house: and every wise husband lets her doeth it."
—Proverbs 14:1 (Pastor George Translation)

My wife is an amazing visionary and multi-tasker. She can run project circles around me. And she sure knows every detail! Her recall ability is absolutely astounding. I can give you a headline or two, but hands down—Terri Copeland Pearsons is definitely the "Detail Queen."

But even more than that, she is a woman of God and a woman of faith. All throughout our wonderful married life, she has been an inspiration to me. Because of her heritage, she taught me how to live by faith and give God's Word first place.

That is exactly why I asked her to join me with this special bonus teaching. We needed to have Terri's "take" on what we did. I wanted you to know—in intimate detail—"Our Personal Journey" of believing God for our homes.

What you are about to read is Terri's account of our walk of faith. She masterfully takes us behind the scenes and shares intimate details that have never been shared publicly. I appreciate the way she laid this out, house by house. There were so many details that I had forgotten when I first read this.

I know this will inspire you as it did me—and I was there!

Read it prayerfully. I believe as you do, revelation for your home will come.

Father, I pray for the ones reading this right now. Open the eyes of their understanding and reveal Your personal plan for their home. Thank You for helping them and encouraging their faith, in Jesus' Name."

Now, let your journey begin as Terri shares ours.

A. **Foundation Scripture for Success in Life—John 4:23:** "A time will come, however, indeed it is already here, when the true (genuine) worshipers will worship the Father in spirit and in truth (reality); for the Father is seeking just such people as these as His worshipers" *(The Amplified Bible)*.

1. First, note that Jesus said, "Thy word is truth" in John 17:17. *The Amplified Bible* defines *truth* as "reality."

   a. When you seek the Word as your reality, it will become real for you. It will actually become what it says it already is. The Word still becomes natural things just like it did in Genesis 1. It is already real in the spirit realm, but it will become real in all aspects of your life.

   b. Those who truly worship the Father are yielding to His Word in their lives.

   c. The Word of God will change your life step by step until you look like Jesus.

2. Second, note the phrase "in spirit." It is the Spirit who leads us in the Word of God, helping us to understand it and how to apply it to our lives. He is the One who shows us how to live by it.

3. John 16:13-15 says, "But when He, the Spirit of Truth (the Truth-giving Spirit) comes, He will guide you into all the Truth (the whole, full Truth). For He will not speak His own message [on His own authority]; but He will tell whatever He hears [from the Father; He will give the message that has been given to Him], and He will announce and declare to you the things that are to come [that will happen in the future]. He will honor and glorify Me, because He will take of (receive, draw upon) what is Mine and will reveal (declare, disclose, transmit) it to you. Everything that the Father has is Mine. That is what I meant when I said that He [the Spirit] will take the things that are Mine and will reveal (declare, disclose, transmit) it to you" *(AMP)*.

4. The Holy Spirit will guide you into all truth. He will point you to the Word, then help you walk out the Word in your life.

5. Give the Word of God first place, making it final authority.

6. I wasn't particularly aware of the verse in John 4, but in retrospect I can see that throughout our lives it was when we were worshiping God in spirit and in truth that our lives increased.

7. *Increase* is a good word to describe what happens when you walk with God by putting His Word first in your life *and* insist on being led by the Spirit.

   a. The word *increase* itself indicates a process. You don't go from beginning to end with no middle. Jesus gave us the kingdom process in Mark 4:28: "First the blade, then the ear, *after* that the full corn in the ear."

   b. 3 John 2 says, "Beloved, I wish above all things that thou mayest prosper and be in health, even as thy soul prospereth."

   c. The ways of God always include prospering and increasing in quality and in quantity.

d. You grow, or develop, in the Word. Paul used the phrase, "skillful in the Word of righteousness." Skill indicates maturing. It means being able to go to the Word of God and take up the Word the Holy Spirit quickens to you as a weapon (Ephesians 6:17).

e. Romans 8:14 says that those who "are led by the Spirit of God, they are the sons of God." Not just children. Not all children. But sons. The Greek word here indicates a maturity. This is talking about being sons, not just children.

f. When you are led by the Holy Spirit there is a natural process of maturing.

g. You are led by the Spirit as you mature. As you mature, you are led more and more by the Spirit.

8. I want to share how this process has worked in our lives. It was in preparing for this broadcast that I realized this is what's been happening over the course of our 36 years of marriage—and is still happening!

9. This isn't only about believing for the house we are currently in, but there have been four other houses. Our going from the first to the fourth house is a good picture of what walking with the Lord looks like—in every area of life, not just in regard to houses.

B. Our First Home

1. Our faith for a house started when we got married.

2. We sought to rent for our first house, with not much vision beyond that.

3. We looked as far away as an hour's drive to the office.

4. I am sure we prayed and asked the Lord for His help, but it wasn't that significant of a faith effort that I remember. It was the blessing of the tither at work for us.

a. We had committed to tithe. We had dedicated our lives to the Lord with all our hearts, but we weren't focused in faith for anything more than a place to live. I don't recall even asking the Lord for specifics for this house.

b. We were seeking the Kingdom and God's will for our lives and that focus took all the faith we had.

c. We had been developing in being led by the Spirit as a couple since our relationship started. We didn't know a lot about going to the Word of God for a house or about seeking to be led *on purpose*.

d. The blessing of being a tither was at work for us, even though we didn't know to make specific requests.

"THE BLESSING OF BEING A TITHER WAS AT WORK FOR US
even though we didn't know to make specific requests."

5. We were seeking the Kingdom and He was faithful to His Word that **He** would add "things" to us (Matthew 6:33), and He did it. We found a rent house that was brand new.

    a. The landlords had built it for her parents, who didn't want it, so they decided to rent it. They were wonderful landlords. It was really cute.

    b. It was only seven minutes from the office, which was wonderful. I was working in the mailroom and George was working in the art department.

    c. The house was 1400 square feet, maybe, including the garage. That's a fairly small house, but we rolled around in it, like a marble in a jar.

        i.   All we had was a kitchen table and chairs, a mattress, a bookshelf my cousin had made, a piano my grandmother gave us, and a very old chair.

        ii. Our clothes were in cardboard boxes when we got married. Praise God, someone gave us a halfway refurbished chest of drawers almost immediately after we were married. (It stayed halfway finished the rest of the time we owned it!)

6. It was at this point that we truly began going to the Word on purpose, not for a house, but for furniture. We prayed the prayer of agreement according to Matthew 18:18-19.

    a. We were seeking the Kingdom. We knew we needed to put action to our faith and we followed the leading of the Spirit.

    b. We marked off space on the floor with masking tape for a couch. We would walk around that space like a couch was there, thanking the Lord for our furniture.

    c. The Lord helped me and I found a set of three tall baskets for $25 that I used as end tables.

    d. I would pray and ask the Lord to show me how to arrange the living room to look fuller, in spite of having hardly any furniture, and He did.

    e. It took a little while, but eventually someone gave us a used couch— it was not my personal taste, but we were really grateful to have something to sit on. After nearly a year we bought our first new couch, and things were starting to look better.

7. We had been married two years and along came baby number one, Jeremy. By the time he was a year and a half old, we had outgrown that house—both inside and out. It was more than the fact that there was little room for us. The Word was growing in us. Without us really thinking about it, or on purpose by faith reaching for a bigger house, the Word in us was producing one for us. The vision it was producing in us was too big for that house anymore.

8. We were seeking the Kingdom and putting the Word first place in our lives. How was the Word first place?

    a. The preaching of the Word was playing in our home all the time. We were in conferences and in church and of course, we read our Bibles.

    b. We were listening to, speaking and applying the Word we heard.

    c. The Word was an integral part of our lives.

9. The same process that brought us to the first house set us up for the second.

C. The Second House

1. Once again, I would say it was the blessing of being a tither that took over for us.

2. Matthew 6:33 says, "But seek ye first the kingdom of God, and his righteousness; and all these things shall be added unto you."

3. We were seeking the Kingdom. Our lives were about seeking Kingdom realities. Being tithers was doing things for us that we didn't even know to ask for. We hadn't taken any action on looking for a house, but we knew it was time to move. Everything changed very quickly.

4. Our grandparents bought a house. Granddad could see the ministry moving north of Fort Worth and wanted to move that direction with it. After they bought it, however, my grandmother wouldn't budge out of her home. So, he wanted us to have the new house.

    a. It all happened in less than a week. I had only seen the house once. He called and asked us to take it. It was a nice brick home, and double the square footage of our current house.

    b. Granddad had paid cash for a sizable portion. He asked that we pay him back directly for that portion and then to assume the loan.

    c. I know for a fact that he didn't ask us to pay back the full portion of what he had paid, so we got a good Granddad deal. That was the blessing of the Lord for a good start.

    d. However, we had to make double payments—one to the loan company and one to him. That lasted for several years.

5. Things were tight, but the Lord helped us. In the natural, we wouldn't have been able to take a vacation, but more than once someone who received free Hawaiian vacations as a trade in business would give us one of those trips. So we weren't suffering—except that we couldn't afford to do anything inside the house. In that way, I was suffering! There are only a few colors that I run from in decorating: orange, rust and brown. This house had rust carpet; orange countertops; and orange, rust and silver wallpaper. I don't ever recall really asking the Lord for help in that area. We just tolerated it (which was help from the Lord in itself).

6. After we paid Granddad back, we were able to start saving for changes in the house. The Lord blessed us, and a little extra came in here and there.

7. When it came to home improvements, I didn't see us with money. I had a mental and spiritual block about believing God.

    a. Eventually, we had enough cash to change a few things that really helped, like carpet and paint in a few rooms. We had been in the house for six years. I remember because when Aubrey was born, I was giving last-minute instructions to the painter from my hospital bed!

    b. About six years later, I found myself really wanting to deal with those orange countertops. The Word had continued to develop a sense of purpose inside me that I wasn't even conscious of. We were busy with the Kingdom in lots of other ways, growing in faith and growing in God. So when the desire rose in me to change my surroundings, I was very much on purpose this time to ask and then believe I received.

8. We were always giving and receiving. Our giving was increasing. We gave that couch the Lord had blessed us with and for some time used lawn furniture in the living room. We cleaned out the kitchen cabinets to help someone else. We gave into ministries and continued sowing into the Kingdom. God was faithful. He always replaced those things with better than what we had. We were living for the Kingdom. Whether it was working or raising our children, we were endeavoring to be led by the Spirit. God always provided for us and prospered us.

9. We were not pastoring at the time, but we were active in church. I was teaching a new-members class when a lady I had never met before came up to me and said, "The Lord has told me to get involved with you on whatever project you are working on." I told her, "My house." She was fine with that and wrote a check to me for several thousand dollars. There was my new flooring and countertops.

10. The Word continued to grow in us over the next six years. Our vision was growing from the inside out and it began to reach for the next place we were to live.

    a. This second house was the kind of house some people live in for their entire lives, but the Word was increasing in us and it was producing an increased vision that just had to get out.

    b. We didn't know exactly what to do except to put action to our faith. We got clear direction and an impression in our spirits to pack up as much of the house as we could. So we did, and for quite some time we lived with stacked boxes and the smell of cardboard; but it was a step that moved us to the next house.

D. The Third House

1. By now we had learned a lot about being on purpose with our faith. We had developed in faith for healing, love, our children, and our role in the ministry. You've heard my dad, Kenneth Copeland, tell about us starting the TV and publications departments, which we did. But by this time the Lord had taken

George from art director, to CEO of KCM, to pastor of the church there on ministry property.

2. We had been pastoring EMIC for about five years when this desire to move had grown in us. Again, this was a result of the Word producing vision and increase in us.

    a. It's the nature of the Word to do that.

    b. The Lord told me, *Did you know you have to believe against the Word for it not to produce in your life?* If you believe you are not supposed to increase in a certain area you can shut down what the Word will automatically do for you.

    c. If you will however, on purpose, focus and set your faith to allow the Word to produce for you in a certain area, it will expedite the results. We were growing in this.

"IF YOU WILL, HOWEVER,
ON PURPOSE,
focus
AND
SET YOUR FAITH
to allow the Word to produce for you in a certain area, it will **EXPEDITE THE RESULTS.**"

3. God is faithful to His Word. God had to move us to get us in position for what He had for us.

4. Three years before, the Lord had let us know that we were to give our house to another family—debt free. We were not debt free at the time, so we began working to pay off the house.

    a. The house was our seed. In the spirit it was sown the moment we determined to give it.

    b. We did a little research and found a few ways to pay the mortgage down. We added to our payments and the Lord helped us.

    c. We knew it would be good to be debt free, but if the Lord hadn't told us to give the house without debt, I don't think we would have pressed into debt freedom the way we did.

    d. Even with our best efforts, we still had a ways to go to completely pay the house off.

5. We received a call from a minister friend who said he had a word from the Lord for our congregation. We fully trusted him and said he could come right away. That Wednesday evening, the word he preached was about how God will bless those who honor Him, His Word and His servants. He spoke of sowing and reaping and then, to our surprise, he received an offering for us for a new house! We hadn't told anyone about wanting to move, other than normal conversation with friends and family. It was a significant offering. The amount exceeded what would normally be expected from a congregation that size.

6. Of course, we immediately used the money to pay off the remainder of the loan. It took 17 years to pay off a 30-year mortgage. Glory to God, the house was paid for! That was a little over half the time it would have taken if we hadn't taken action. Thankfully, we had a little of the offering left over to help us get into the next house.

7. Yet, there was a mental and spiritual block in us for the next house, as we couldn't see ourselves living beyond our current part of town (and standard of living). The Lord had to help us.

8. As soon as the house was paid off, we gave it to the family the Lord had told us to three years before. The problem was, we had no place to go. So, to be honorable, since we had given the house, we paid rent to the new owners until we could find a house.

9. That was another place to use our faith—finding a house.

   a. The power of increase was strong in me, yet I didn't really know what it looked like. The Lord knew we needed to "come up." Just like He took Abraham outside and showed him the stars, He took us somewhere to help us begin to see what His blessing could look like for us.

   b. We were invited to some friends' house for a Christmas party. They had just moved to town, so we had not yet seen their house. They lived quite a distance from us. Their house was beautiful, with quality and class. The neighborhood was grand and uplifting—a feast for your eyes.

   c. George stood on the sidewalk, looked around the neighborhood and said, "This is too rich for my blood." But the seed of faith in the Word had been planted, and it grew very quickly.

10. The Word was producing something bigger on the inside than we could see on the outside. We were being conformed to the Word.

    a. God was obligated to do what the Word was producing in us. God wanted to bless us.

    b. The Word in you will demand better. The Word brings increase.

    c. The Word produced a massive harvest in our lives.

11. Obviously, our heads had no idea what to look for—and on top of that, we didn't know where to look for it. Our thinking was limited, but the Lord was helping us to come up to the level the Word had brought our spirits.

    a. I was following the witness of the Spirit. We looked at dozens of houses. It was all part of the process of the Lord bringing us to what He had for us.

    b. After a couple of months of looking, the realtor said, "You have looked at every house on the market in this area. You are going to have to go outside this radius." I was apprehensive about that, and couldn't really "see" it.

12. The same minister friend called us again and said, "I was praying and it seems to me that you are not looking out far enough for your house. It's farther away." That's when freedom dropped into my spirit and I could see us moving outside our comfort zone, living somewhere beyond where I had been thinking.

13. We only looked at a few houses before the realtor took us to the most beautiful house I had ever been in. Every detail was impressive: crown moldings, woodwork, tile, appliances. The yard, the neighborhood, even the gas stations in the area were pretty. Remember the lady who gave me several thousand dollars some six years before? She and her husband were with us. After looking at that house for an hour, we danced on the front porch. This was it. Faith friends are a true blessing of the Lord.

14. We looked down the street just a few houses, and there was the house we had visited for a Christmas party only a few months before. There was the sidewalk where George had told the Lord that this neighborhood was "too rich for his blood." The goodness of the Lord had helped us again. He was faithful to His Word.

15. So we bought the house. That was miraculous. We had given our house, so we had no income from that, but we did have some left from the special offering that had been received for us. With some fancy footwork with the mortgage company, we were able to borrow the money.

16. Yes, we went from debt free back to debt owed. We wanted to be debt free, and thought it was a good idea to be debt free, but didn't fully understand that we *needed* to be debt free. We couldn't comprehend that.

17. Dad had been preaching about God's provision for debt freedom, but not as intensely as he is now. He was very kind and supportive, and told us from the very start that we needed to believe to get out of debt as soon as we could. We'd had some success in that area already, so we were ready for that challenge.

18. What we had faith for, the Lord gave us.

    a. We had faith for the ability to not only make the payments but to maintain the house. And that was a lot, financially. The yard itself was labor-intensive.

    b. I determined, because the Lord was putting it in us, that we were not going to let one thing wait that needed attention. And sure enough, what we purposed our faith for, the Lord provided. We never slacked in any area of that house.

    c. We had faith for furniture, and that was a good thing. A neighbor came to greet us after a couple of weeks and said, "Oh, your furniture hasn't arrived yet?" I told her it was coming. We were back to rolling around in the house like a marble in a jar. We believed God and we were sowing seed. We had given away nearly all the furniture we owned, and it was nice furniture.

19. Now this was not God's best. How could being thousands of dollars in debt be His best? Not by far.

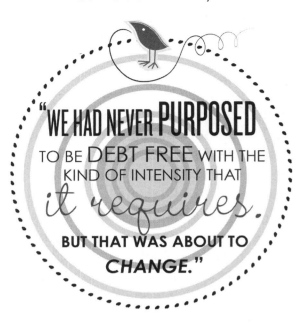

"WE HAD NEVER **PURPOSED** TO BE **DEBT FREE** WITH THE KIND OF INTENSITY THAT *it requires.* BUT THAT WAS ABOUT TO **CHANGE.**"

   a. Praise God for Psalm 103:11 that says His mercy is toward those who fear Him. I asked the Lord, "What does that really mean?" He said, *If you are looking to honor the Lord, even your mistakes will work out.*

   b. Some may think, *Well, I'll just go ahead and do it and deal with it later. The Lord will fix it.* No. That's not the fear of the Lord. That does not honor His Word. If you take that approach you will have more to overcome than debt. It will set you back in so many ways and show up all across your life. Some may never recover because it is self-deception.

20. So, here we were, borrowers again and servants to the lenders. We were subject to people we did not know. Again, we wanted to be debt free, but we didn't see that we *needed* to be debt free.

21. Romans 13:8 says, "Owe no man any thing, but to love one another: for he that loveth another hath fulfilled the law." This wasn't a revelation to us yet, but God was faithful to bring us to that point. We had never purposed to be debt free with the kind of intensity that it requires. But that was about to change.

22. Not long after we had moved into our house, change began in George during a 30 Days of Glory meeting. These are his comments:

   a. Sept. 12, 1998, Brother Copeland spent an entire service preaching about staying out of debt and suddenly my eyes were opened.

   b. "What one does today for the sake of tomorrow is called an investment. What one does to enjoy today at the expense of tomorrow is called debt." —Kenneth Copeland

   c. "Borrowing is a replacement covenant—it is going to someone else when you should have gone to God." —Kenneth Copeland

   d. I realized borrowing had become a serious breach of my covenant with God.

   e. Kenneth asked me to do a week of broadcasts with him about being debt free. On one of the broadcasts, Kenneth looked at me and asked, "You got out of debt and then you got back into debt. Why did you do that?" It felt like all of the air left the studio. I remember a camera operator peering around the side of her camera at us as I fumbled, attempting to answer. The Lord had told Brother Copeland to ask me that question. It made me determined and on fire to be debt free.

23. The Lord led the children of Israel out of the land of Egypt. He began to lead us too, and a transformation occurred.

24. A shift took place in us. Our view of debt changed. The Word of God was conforming us to His will.

    a. We drove past the place where we had signed the mortgage papers and without thinking I pointed at it and said, "That is where we committed that awful sin." Now, borrowing was a sin to us. It wasn't before. We didn't have vision for it. But we did now.

25. "The very moment you make the quality decision to live debt free, God sees you debt free. All you need to do now is walk this out by faith, believe God's Word and be obedient to whatever He tells you to do." —Kenneth Copeland

26. I don't know what it would have looked like to have believed God for a house without debt. It would have been good. It would have been better. But the Lord is so kind and so good, He helped us. He walked us into it.

27. When we moved into the house, I had an inner sense that led me to believe we would only live in this house for about three years. It was actually four, but what did happen in three years was the knowing that we were to move back to the area we had lived in for 17 years.

"A SHIFT TOOK PLACE IN US. OUR VIEW OF DEBT CHANGED. THE WORD OF GOD WAS CONFORMING US TO HIS WILL."

28. During those three years, the Lord ingrained in us a new and higher standard for living.

    a. We were surrounded with quality and beauty.

    b. It took those three years for us to see ourselves in that kind of environment and for that environment to be in us to the degree it could be reproduced someplace else.

29. By now, our purpose in faith was stronger than it had ever been. I had learned so much about being led by the inner witness of the Spirit. We had watched the Lord provide for us, and we were making good progress on getting rid of the debt.

a. For the next year we set our faith and ALL our efforts to pay it off—and we did!

b. It took 17 years to pay off the house we eventually sowed, but now, a house that was worth four times as much was paid off in only four years!

c. The seed of the Word was working in our lives.

30. We were determined to be in God's will, in the perfect house, in the right location and debt free. That determination took us to the Word at a whole new level. And the Word, along with being led by the Spirit, took us to our next home.

E. The Fourth House

1. So, here we were, again needing a place to live. This time we were smarter, and we set time aside to seek the Lord in His Word and His leading.

2. We took three days away to pray about nothing else. We prayed and sought the Lord until the afternoon, and then we enjoyed each other and reflected on our prayer time.

   a. The Lord spoke to us. He gave us three things:

      i. He reassured us that there was a house for us. (Remember, we were moving back to the area where the realtor had told us we had seen every house available.)

      ii. He told us to not be afraid to remodel and to add on. I had struggled with that kind of thing in the past, but the Lord helped me through the decorating process of the house we were in. He told me that the house would have "personality."

      iii. He told us not to put the house we were in on the market until we had found the one we were going to live in.

3. It turned out that a house owned by a relative was for sale—it was a nice house but was not my style. It was only a little over half the size of the one we were living in. It was not what I thought I was looking for, but the Lord spoke.

   a. Two phone calls came. One was from Gloria and she said, "Terri, I think that house is your house." Another call came from a friend who had never been in the house but knew it was for sale. She said the same thing.

> "The very moment you make the
>
> ## QUALITY DECISION
> to live debt free, God sees you debt free.
>
>
>
> All you need to do now is walk this out *by faith,* believe God's Word and be obedient to whatever He tells you to do."
> —Kenneth Copeland

b. Two phone calls were not enough to make me take action, but it was enough to look within. Now, when I looked at the house naturally, it was not what I needed or wanted; but when I turned inward, I found peace. "Let peace...act as umpire" (Colossians 3:15, *The Amplified Bible*).

c. From that moment, we began a journey that took us step by step through a five-year process of a massive remodel. But it was five years of miracles and blessing. My, what we saw the Lord do. But, the greatest part of it all was the way our walk with Him increased. *That's the heart of what faith is all about—walking with Him.*

"FROM THAT MOMENT, WE BEGAN A JOURNEY THAT TOOK US STEP BY STEP THROUGH A FIVE-YEAR PROCESS OF A MASSIVE REMODEL. BUT IT WAS FIVE YEARS OF MIRACLES AND BLESSINGS.

4. The difference this time from all the times before was that we were really putting the Word first place. We looked to it for everything—starting with the location. Deuteronomy 12:11 (plus Deuteronomy 12:18 and 16:6, 15) speaks of the place that the Lord had chosen to put His Name, for His presence to dwell. He had led us to our place. We looked up scriptures about Abraham who was looking for a city whose builder and maker was God (Hebrews 11:10). We confessed those verses and we released faith that we were being led.

5. The first thing He did was give us a plan. We hadn't sold our house yet, so we agreed to buy this house, but we needed the owners to let us "rent" from them until our house was sold. They did and as soon as our house sold, we paid cash for their house. Debt free again!

6. I knew I had to make changes in the house for it to work for us. I needed much more storage, and I wanted other additions, like an office for myself.

   a. We started with an approach to make a few adjustments, but that is not what the Lord wanted. There was a vision the Lord had been working in me for nearly 30 years and it was scratching to get out. I was so agitated. I would start to settle for something because of cost or time, and the scratching inside would not let me do it. This scratching wouldn't let me tolerate things that didn't match the vision God had given me on the inside.

   b. After already working on the remodel for a few months, I became so agitated because I knew things weren't right. I stopped everything and again sought the Lord. We shut down any work for four months. We had expected to be in a rent house during this process for only six months. We would now see that was not going to happen. It was a great time to develop patience.

7. There was a key that really got the whole process moving again. The Lord put it in my heart to honor George. All he had ever expressed a desire for was an office with a view of the water, one that was designed in a New England style. That made sense since he was raised on Cape Cod. While this house is not on the lake, it is across the street from ones that are. I asked the architect what we could do. He put a tall ladder outside the house and climbed up, and discovered that from a second story we could see the lake. But there was no second-story portion of the house that could be George's office. Unbeknown to me, the leading of the Holy Spirit was beginning a domino effect that took us down an amazing path: *Just add on to the master bath a few feet and go up a story.*

   a. The effect of the Holy Spirit was phenomenal. We would pray in the spirit until an answer came, and it always did.

   b. We went from little, to closets galore. When we took out a bookcase that was agitating me, we discovered space enough for a walk-in storage closet and a walk-in cedar closet! We took in the driveway on one side of the house, bumped about 4 feet on the other end and connected the roofline. Little did we know that would give us a third floor! In addition, by connecting the roofline we were able to make way for a new staircase to the second floor and to George's office. As we connected the new section to the old, we discovered an enormous amount of space already under the roof that simply needed to be finished out. Included was an area that I made our Christmas storage room, large enough for all our Christmas decorations, including our trees, which we are able to leave standing!

   c. One time, the Lord spoke to my heart and said, *Believe Me for a dining room.* That sounded crazy; I had a dining room. But I had learned to be led. The room that was supposed to be a dining room was really too small for our family and through a process of planning and then replanning, I finally realized what was just a big, open room was supposed to be our dining room, and the other room was to be our music room. Oh, the joy of being led.

8. We had to be willing to listen, to learn, and sometimes redo. That scratching on the inside would not let me shortchange the vision.

9. All along, we were putting the Word first. We focused on the Word on a level we had never done before. We went to the Word for every element—for foundations, sinks, floors, walls, fabrics, light fixtures—and we found some cool ones. George found many of them in 1 Kings 6 and 7.* We discovered that God loves house design! We made confession cards and were speaking the scriptures, believing and receiving His perfect design for our house. Once we had stripped the existing sheetrock and reframed walls the way

we wanted, we invited friends to write confessions from scripture on the studs that pertained to the rooms they were going in.** The Word became doorknobs, paint, light fixtures and everything we needed!

    a. The testimony about our light fixtures was outstanding. Our decorator found a tent sale with designer light fixtures, including chandeliers and even a Waterford-crystal sconce. We paid about 10 cents on the dollar.

    b. Things like that were happening all the time. Money was coming in from unexpected sources. It was truly miraculous.

10. Even though the actual add-on footprint was small, we more than doubled the square footage of the house.

11. What an amazing journey it was, and still is.

F. Your Journey

1. Your journey involves a stand of faith. There is a home for you. There is debt freedom for you. The same Word that produced a vision for us, house by house, will produce for you.

2. Sometimes the journey is as important as the destination, if the journey is a walk with the Lord and not just a desire for "stuff." Walk with the Lord and "stuff" will follow.

3. As you walk out the Word of God and walk in His precepts and His way of doing things, you will prosper. Through faith and patience you will obtain the promises.

*Pastor George's House Scriptures from 1 Kings 6-7, NIV

The temple that King Solomon built for the LORD was sixty cubits long, twenty wide and thirty high. The portico at the front of the main hall of the temple extended the width of the temple, that is twenty cubits, and projected ten cubits from the front of the temple. He made narrow windows high up in the temple walls. Against the walls of the main hall and inner sanctuary he built a structure around the building, in which there were side rooms. The lowest floor was five cubits wide, the middle floor six cubits and the third floor seven. He made offset ledges around the outside of the temple so that nothing would be inserted into the temple walls (6:2-6).

On the walls all around the temple, in both the inner and outer rooms, he carved cherubim, palm trees and open flowers. He also covered the floors of both the inner and outer rooms of the temple with gold (6:29-30).

All these structures, from the outside to the great courtyard and from foundation to eaves, were made of blocks of high-grade stone cut to size and smoothed on their inner and outer faces. The foundations were laid with large stones of good quality, some measuring ten cubits and some eight. Above were high-grade stones, cut to size, and cedar beams (7:9-11).

He then made ten bronze basins, each holding forty baths and measuring four cubits across, one basin to go on each of the ten stands. He placed five of the stands on the south side of the temple and five on the north. He placed the Sea on the south side, at the southeast corner of the temple. He also made the pots and shovels and sprinkling bowls.... (7:38-40).

**Scriptures Friends Wrote on Our House (paraphrased)

There, of course, were many others. But the search for God's Word to YOU is, perhaps, the richest part of the journey. The Holy Spirit knows how to lead you. Armed with that knowledge and a good concordance you will discover an endless treasure of scriptures coming to life for you.

Front Entry:

Song of Solomon 2:4: "His banner over me is love."

Psalm 37:23: "The steps of a good man are ordered of the Lord."

For the Kitchen:

Deuteronomy 28:5: "Blessed shall be your basket and your kneading bowl."

Ecclesiastes 9:7: "Go your way, eat your bread with joy."

Psalm 103:5: "He satisfies your mouth with good things."

Behind the Refrigerator:

Romans 12:21: "Do not let yourselves be overcome by evil." (A personal favorite!)

Windows:

Ecclesiastes 11:7: "Truly the light is sweet and a pleasant thing it is for the eyes to behold."

By the Electrical Power Box:

Acts 1:8: "You shall receive power."

Matthew 5:14: "You are the light of the world. A city that is set on a hill cannot be hid."

Pastor's Study:

Proverbs 14:33: "Wisdom is at home in the mind of one who has understanding."

Psalm 5:3: "My voice shall You hear in the morning."

Psalm 119:68: "Teach me thy statues."

Bedroom:

Psalm 4:8: "I will both lay me down in peace and sleep for thou, Lord, only makest me dwell in safety."

Children's Room:

Isaiah 54:13: "Your children shall be disciples taught of the Lord and obedient to His will and great shall be the peace and undisturbed composure of your children."

DIVINE PROSPERITY

Chapter 3 *from* **God's Will Is Prosperity**
by Gloria Copeland

The first thing I began to believe God for was a home. But what about Romans 13:8? It says that we are to owe no man anything but to love him. How can you believe God for enough money to buy a home? This is one area most people think impossible. Many have made the statement, "Surely you don't have to believe for a home without borrowing money!"

You certainly don't have to, but I happen to know it works. Of course, Satan told me that there was no way I could have a home without borrowing money for it. That is the world's way and what everyone is expected to do, but I refused to believe Satan. We had made an irrevocable commitment—we were not going to borrow money. Believing God was the *only way* I could have my home.

When Satan would come at me with doubt and unbelief, this is one verse I trusted in. I confessed it continually, and it gave me comfort and strength to stand in faith. Second Corinthians 9:8, *The Amplified Bible*, says, "And God is able to make all grace (every favor and earthly blessing) come to you in abundance, so that you may always and under all circumstances and whatever the need be self-sufficient [possessing enough to require no aid or support and furnished in abundance for every good work and charitable donation]."

> "BELIEVING GOD
> WAS THE
> *only way*
> I COULD HAVE
> MY HOME."

Satan would come at me with thoughts of doubt and say, "There is no way you are going to have your needs met. There is no way you can buy a house without going into debt. There is just no way!" I would answer him with, "No, Satan, my God is able!" *I hung my faith on that scripture.*

The Word says that He is able to get it to you. Don't look to natural sources. Don't look to your job. When you are believing God, you have to look to His Word. *Keep your eye single on the Word.* You have to realize and know that He can and will work in your behalf. God is a real operator! He is able to get things done!

So, we started believing God years ago for the home we have now. We could have borrowed the money years sooner, but we refused to compromise on our decision. Whenever there is a choice between the world's way and the Word's way, we always go with the Word. The world's system may seem to be the easier way, but we refuse to go the way of the world. In the long run, God's way is not only easier but far superior. He has certainly proven that to us.

We began believing God for the perfect home when we lived in Tulsa, Oklahoma, in 1968. At the same time, there was a lady in Forth Worth, Texas, who started building her home. She had the plans drawn and saw to the purchasing of materials personally.

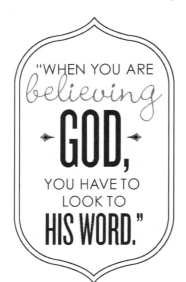
"WHEN YOU ARE *believing* GOD, YOU HAVE TO LOOK TO HIS WORD."

It was several years before I saw that home, but the floor plan was exactly what we needed to meet our needs as a family. In addition to the living space, there was a study in the back of the house—a place away from the living area where we could study the Word and write. It was perfect for us. She began to build it at the very time we began to believe for it!

God started to work immediately. There was no evidence of that for us to see, but we had learned to look to the Word for evidence and not to the circumstances.

When we first looked at the house, we were on our way to the airport to leave town. Really, at first I didn't know exactly what I had in mind. As I thought about the house over the next few days, the Lord started showing me things I could do to it. The house had stayed empty for months. It seemed that nobody could live there. The owners were just trying to get rid of it. They had given it away once but got it back. They couldn't even give it away! That was our home!

When I believe God for something, I don't waver. I have made a quality decision that the Word is true. I have built into myself a reliance on God's Word. I believe His Word more than I believe what I can see or feel. I know that God is able and He will get it to me. As I have heard Kenneth Hagin say, "If you are determined to stand forever, it won't take very long." That's the way I am when I am believing God for something. I could stand forever if necessary.

We leased the house for one year. We agreed to pay cash for it at the end of that year. Our needs had always been met abundantly. We lived well. We did what we wanted to do. But as far as having that much money in cash, we just didn't have it and never had. In the natural there was no reason to expect to have it, but in the spirit we knew our God was able. When we moved in, the house was in need of repair.

It needed to be completely remodeled, so I was faced with a decision. I had enough money to start the remodeling because I had saved some money to buy a home when I found one; but I thought, *This is not our home legally. It would really be unwise to put thousands of dollars into a house that doesn't even belong to us.* What was I supposed to do? At that point, I had to act on my faith. I decided that it was my house—I had believed that I received it. I had put my foot on that place, and it was mine in the Name of Jesus. As an act of faith, I went to work, calling in people to start remodeling. During that year Satan said, "Well, that sure is a lot of money for you to lose."

But I would answer, "No, in the Name of Jesus, this is my house and it will be paid for in July. We will pay cash for it. I believe we have the money in the Name of Jesus!"

Whenever God called us to do something in the ministry, we always had to believe Him for the money before we could start. Because we wouldn't borrow money, we had to wait until we had the cash. When we went into television, we believed God for the money first before we actually started production. In the radio ministry, we did the same thing. We might have to believe God for six months before the money would come into our hands. That is how we had always operated. During that year, the ministry was growing and stretching out; the payroll was growing. We always had enough to meet the budget, but it was nip and tuck. There never was anything much left over.

Paying cash for a home is a challenge to faith. We had by faith stepped into a situation that certainly was beyond our natural ability or means. We were trusting the Word of God to perform and accomplish our goal, and the Word came to our rescue with further revelation! We were committed to God's Word, and God was committed to us. We had taken the step of faith, and God saw to it that we had the revelation knowledge of His Word to put us over. I am convinced beyond doubt that our commitment years before to stay out of debt made the difference. If we had not committed to God's Word then, we would not know what we know today about God's system of finance. We would not be able to share these things with you, and today we would be living far below our privileges as believers.

A DIVINE REVELATION

One day as I was standing in my house looking out the window and thinking about these things, God gave me what I would call a revelation of *divine prosperity*. I realized that we had been looking at finances and prosperity in a different way from other things, such as divine health. If a symptom of sickness came on my body, I would not stand for it. I would take authority over it immediately and not allow it to remain. By doing this, I walk in divine health. I am convinced that healing and divine health belong to me in the New Covenant.

"God started to work
IMMEDIATELY."

"There was no evidence
of that for us to see,
but we had learned
to look to

the Word

for evidence and
not to the circumstances."

Divine prosperity works exactly the same way, but we had not been using the Word to believe for divine prosperity as we had for divine health. We had been living in the laws of prosperity for years, but we had been acting on prosperity differently from other provisions of the Word in this way: *We would allow symptoms of lack to come on us and stay there. We were willing to tolerate them.* When the Lord began to deal with me on this, He made me realize that Jesus bore the curse of poverty at the same time He bore the curse of sickness. I already knew it, but I saw that I was not acting on it to the fullest. You can believe for divine prosperity just as you believe for divine health. Both blessings already belong to you. You should refuse lack just as quickly as you refuse sickness.

"JESUS PAID THE PRICE
FOR YOUR SICKNESS.
IT IS NOT A PROMISE.
It's a fact.
IT HAS ALREADY BEEN DONE."

There was a time when we knew that praying for the sick was a valid thing. When we got sick, we would pray, and most of the time we would get healed. We knew that healing was for us. We knew it was real, so we believed God for healing when we got sick. But when we heard through Kenneth Hagin that Jesus bore our sicknesses and carried our diseases and by His stripes we were healed, the situation was changed in our lives concerning healing. We didn't wait until we got sick to believe God for healing. We decided to walk in divine health because we *were* healed 2,000 years ago when Jesus paid the price.

I remember the night we heard that we *were* healed by the stripes of Jesus. We realized then that we didn't have to be sick anymore. Getting healed when you are sick is great, but staying healed—walking in divine health—is much greater. To get healed is wonderful, but it is much better to realize that Jesus paid for our sicknesses and that we are free from them. He made us free from sickness, and Satan cannot put anything on us without our consent. It may be a consent of ignorance, but nevertheless, you are willing to let him do it. He can't affect you unless you let him.

Jesus paid the price for your sickness. It is not a promise. It is a fact. It has already been done. We need to see prosperity in the same light that we see healing and health. He bore the curse of poverty. We should always have enough. Jesus provided it for us. If you are in lack, if you don't have enough to get by, if you don't have anything extra to invest in the work of the gospel, then you are in an area of poverty—you are suffering symptoms of lack.

Isaiah 1:19 says, "If ye be *willing* and obedient, ye shall eat the good of the land." The word *willing* has become a passive word in our thinking. Actually, in this scripture *willing* is an action word. It involves a decision. If I said, "I am *willing* to live in divine health," I wouldn't just mean, "Well, if somebody slaps it on me, I'll live in it." No. If I am *willing*, I have made up my mind to live that way. I have determined, "I *will* live in divine health. I'm not *willing* to be sick."

If you make up your mind—make a quality decision—that you are not willing to live in lack but that you are willing to live in divine prosperity and abundance, Satan cannot stop the flow of God's financial blessings. If you are willing and obedient, you shall eat the good of the land. Divine prosperity will come to pass in your life. You have exercised your faith in the covenant that you have with God. You have opened the door for Him to establish His covenant with you.

It takes the same kind of decision regarding divine prosperity that it takes for divine health. To walk in divine health, you begin with a decision to no longer allow Satan to put sickness on you; and Satan loses dominion over your body. Frankly, I am just not willing to be sick. I am willing to be well! Jesus paid the price for me, and I am taking advantage of it. In honor of His sacrifice, I will not accept anything less than divine health.

In the same way, I am not *willing* to live in lack. If I thought abundance was not in agreement with God's will, or if I thought that the Word of God did not provide abundance, I would simply leave it alone. But the Word does provide prosperity and abundance for me. I am an heir to the blessing of Abraham. Redemption from the curse of poverty is part of Jesus' substitutionary work at Calvary. He paid the price for *my* prosperity—a heavy price. I will not scorn any part of His work. I deeply appreciate every benefit that His sacrifice provided for me.

 "ONCE YOU MAKE THE DECISION TO RECEIVE WHAT JESUS HAS ALREADY PROVIDED FOR YOU TO WALK IN BIBLE PROSPERITY, SATAN CANNOT STOP YOU FROM BEING PROSPEROUS."

Once you make the decision to receive what Jesus has already provided for you and to walk in Bible prosperity, Satan cannot stop you from being prosperous. When you made the decision to make Jesus the Lord of your life according to Romans 10:9-10, there was no devil in hell that could stop your salvation from coming to pass. Satan and all of his cohorts could not even slow it down. Salvation was being offered; and when you made the decision to receive it, salvation immediately became yours and you became a new creature in Christ Jesus. There was no struggle. Salvation was offered and you took it! So it is with Bible prosperity. You begin to walk in divine prosperity with a decision to no longer allow Satan to put symptoms of lack on you.

Make this quality decision concerning your prosperity: "God's blessing of prosperity belongs to me. I *will* receive it. The symptoms of lack have no right to operate against me." Make this decision and you will begin to enjoy the financial blessing that has belonged to you since you became a believer in Jesus Christ.

REDEEMED FROM THE CURSE

Deuteronomy 28 describes the curse of the law. You can see from these verses that poverty is included in this curse: "And you shall grope at noonday as the blind grope in darkness. And you shall not prosper in your ways; and you shall be only oppressed and robbed continually, and there shall be no one to save you...you shall build a house, but not live in it.... A nation which you have not known shall eat up the fruit of your land and of all your labors, and you shall be only oppressed and crushed continually.... He [the stranger] shall lend to you, but you shall not lend to him; he shall be the head, and you shall be the tail. All these curses shall come upon you and shall pursue you and overtake you" (Deuteronomy 28:29-30, 33, 44-45, *The Amplified Bible*).

From these verses we can plainly see that poverty and lack are a part of the curse of the law. Galatians 3:13-14 very simply says, "Christ hath redeemed us from the curse of the law, being made a curse for us: for it is written, Cursed is every one that hangeth on a tree: that the blessing of Abraham might come on the Gentiles through Jesus Christ." The blessing of Abraham definitely included a financial blessing. The curse of the law definitely included financial reversal.

Galatians 3:13 is one of the verses that caused healing to be a reality in our lives. We knew beyond a doubt that sickness and disease were under the curse and that healing was a part of the blessing of Abraham. Now we can use the same scripture to make divine prosperity a reality in our lives. Jesus redeemed us from the curse of poverty. He redeemed us from every curse of the law.

If we are willing and obedient, the blessing of Abraham will come on us and overtake us. God will multiply us exceedingly and make us exceedingly fruitful. Lack should be a thing of the past, and abundance—more than you can see any way to use—should be the order of the day.

"JESUS REDEEMED US FROM THE CURSE OF POVERTY. HE REDEEMED US FROM EVERY CURSE OF THE LAW."

PEACE AND PROSPERITY

Another scripture that has meant so much to us with regard to healing is Isaiah 53:5, *The Amplified Bible:* "But He was wounded for our transgressions, He was bruised for our guilt and iniquities; the chastisement [needful to obtain] peace and well-being for us was upon Him, and with the stripes [that wounded] Him we are healed and made whole." This says that Jesus bore the "chastisement needful to obtain peace and well-being." Peace and well-being include whatever you need. You can't enjoy peace and well-being if you don't have your needs met. Isaiah 48:18, *The Amplified Bible,* ties the two together, "Oh, that you had hearkened to My commandments! Then your peace and prosperity would have been like a flowing river." Peace and well-being include a prosperous life. God told Abram, "Fear not, Abram, I am your Shield, your abundant compensation, and your reward shall be exceedingly great" (Genesis 15:1, *The Amplified Bible).* Abundant compensation is far-reaching. Abundant compensation means everything. It enveloped Abraham in a blanket of well-being.

"PEACE AND WELL-BEING INCLUDE A *prosperous* LIFE."

Peace and prosperity go hand in hand. Your prosperity has already been provided for you. I pray this will become a reality to you today. Prosperity is yours! It is not something you have to strive to work toward. *You have a titled deed to prosperity.* Jesus bought and paid for your prosperity just as He bought and paid for your healing and your salvation. He bore the curse of sin, of sickness, and of poverty. When He paid the price for sin, He also paid the price for the curse of poverty so that you can be free.

Once you realize that this prosperity *already* belongs to you, you will be in a different position. You will no longer be seeking to obtain it, hoping to get it, or working toward it. You won't have to work toward it because the Word says it is yours now. The Word is your source in prosperity just as it is in healing.

Treat any symptom of lack just as you would treat a symptom of sickness. The very moment a symptom of lack shows up in your life, take authority over it. Command it to flee from you in the Name of Jesus and stand your ground. Say, "Lack, I resist you in the Name of Jesus. I command you to flee from me. I have been redeemed from the curse of poverty and lack. *I will not tolerate you in my life."* Don't allow Satan to steal from you. He will attempt to put symptoms of lack on you, but if you stand on the Word of God, knowing that prosperity belongs to you, he cannot maintain an attack. The Word says that when you resist Satan, he has to flee from you. He has no choice! (see James 4:7.)

DOMINION

Divine prosperity and abundance belong to you now. We, as born-again believers, have the same authority over the earth that Adam had in the Garden of Eden. Look at Genesis 1:27, 28, *The Amplified Bible:* "So God created man in His own image, in the image and likeness of God He created him; male and female He created them. And God blessed them and said to them, Be fruitful, multiply, and fill the earth, and subdue it [using all its vast resources in the service of God and man]; and have dominion over the fish of the sea, the birds of the air, and over every living creature that moves upon the earth." God made the earth, and then He made man and gave man dominion and authority over the earth. It was man's earth (Psalm 115:16). God didn't say, "I will subdue it for you." He said, "You subdue it and have dominion over its vast resources."

While we were standing in faith for the money to pay for our first house, the Lord reminded me of this scripture and revealed to me that every material thing here came from the earth's vast resources. Every piece of lumber, brick, glass, concrete, mortar— there was nothing in the makeup of our house that had not come from the earth's resources. "Be fruitful, multiply, and fill the earth, and subdue it with all its vast resources and have dominion." Anything that you can see with your eyes comes from the earth's resources. (I had not thought about that even though it is obvious that it does.) Every jet airplane is made from material that comes from the earth's resources. Cars, buildings, furniture, jewels, food, clothes, every greenback dollar bill, silver, and gold are products of the earth's vast resources. You cannot have a material need that the earth's resources cannot handle. The raw materials may change, but the substance that gives material things their form comes from the resources of the earth! Glory to God!

God told Adam to subdue the earth and its resources. He gave Adam authority over it. Adam gave that authority to Satan. Then Jesus came to earth, paid the price, and recaptured that authority from Satan. Jesus, in turn, gave that authority to the believer. "And Jesus came and spake unto them, saying, All power is given unto me in heaven and in earth. Go ye therefore, and teach all nations, baptizing them in the name of the Father, and of the Son, and of the Holy Ghost: Teaching them to observe all things whatsoever I have commanded you: and, lo, I am with you always, even unto the end of the world" (Matthew 28:18-20).

I began to see that I already had authority over that house and authority over the money I needed to purchase it. I said, "In the Name of Jesus, I take authority over the money I need. (I called for the specific amount.) I command you to come to me. I take my place, and I take dominion over that which I need. I command it to come in Jesus' Name. Ministering spirits, you go and cause it to come." (Speaking of angels, Hebrews 1:14 says, "Are they not all ministering spirits, sent forth to minister for them who shall be heirs of salvation?" You have angels assigned to minister for you. Psalm 103:20 says that the angels hearken to the voice of God's Word. When you become the voice of God in the earth by putting His Words in your mouth, you put your angels to work! They are highly trained, capable helpers. They know how to get the job done.)

I wasn't taking authority over something that belonged to someone else. That house was up for sale. The people had relinquished their authority when they put it on the market. I had the right to take authority over it and receive it as mine in the Name of Jesus.

Stand your ground on the Word of God simply because it is yours. Believe it and the things you need will come into your life. Take authority over them and command them to come to you in the Name of Jesus. Command the money you need to come to you. The authority is yours. Have dominion and subdue the earth and its vast resources.

Mark 10:29-30 tells us a hundredfold return is available to the giver, but it says that you will receive your return "with persecutions." Persecution simply means that Satan will try you. Persecution has no authority over you. It has no power, but Satan is allowed to test you in that area. He will lie to you and steal from you if he can. He will show you convincing symptoms of lack and tell you, "There is no way." Remember those four words *there is no way* always come from Satan. God will never tell you there is no way. Jesus said, "I am the way." The only way to successfully combat Satan is with the Word of God and the Name of Jesus.

It was six years from the time we started believing God for our first home until we moved into it. At the end of the year's lease, we paid cash for our "faith house." I am still not sure how, except by faith in God's Word. Had we borrowed the money, we would have still had 35 years to

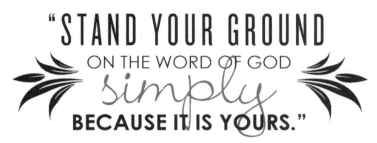

pay! When you think about that, six years does not seem so long. Remember that in 1968 we had hardly scratched the surface of revelation knowledge. We had just realized that faith works. We did not know *how* God's system of prosperity worked. Since then we have learned and are still learning. The next house we paid cash for some years later was many times more expensive and we had the cash in three weeks. Today, just our television bill is well over one million dollars *every* month. How could we borrow enough money each month to pay for that? Thank God, borrowed money is not our source—HE IS!

You cannot receive these things just because I tell you about them. You have to take the scriptures on prosperity and meditate on them until they become a reality in your heart, until you know prosperity belongs to you. Once you have a revelation of divine prosperity in your spirit, you won't allow Satan to take it from you. *The Word of God is the source of your prosperity.* The Word is the source of everything you need in life. "Faith comes by hearing, and hearing by the Word of God." Don't look to people to meet your needs. Look to the Word. Satan will try to convince you that you can never walk in prosperity, but don't look at the circumstances around you. Look at the Word that says it is yours. Don't look to people to meet your needs. Look to the Word. Satan will try to convince you that you can never walk in prosperity, but don't look at the circumstances around you. Look at the Word that says it is yours.

There are different areas of poverty just as there are different areas of sickness. A headache is one thing; terminal cancer is another. I wouldn't enjoy either of them. In the same way, you can have lack in some areas or you can have total lack: You can be without food to eat or without quite enough to make ends meet. Again. I wouldn't enjoy either one.

Why should I? Why should I settle for only a part of the blessing of Abraham? The Word says I am entitled to all the blessing of Abraham.

Don't just believe God to meet your needs. Believe Him for a surplus of prosperity so that you can help others. We here in America are a blessed people financially. We have been called to finance the gospel to the world. According to 2 Corinthians 9:8, *The Amplified Bible,* we should be "self-sufficient [possessing enough to require no aid or support and furnished in abundance for every good work and charitable donation]." Verse 11 says, "Thus you will be enriched in all things and in every way, so that you can be generous...." Isn't that better than just barely getting by?

If you are *furnished in abundance,* then you will be able to reach out to others. You will live in a surplus of prosperity. You will walk in divine prosperity.

"THE WORD OF GOD IS THE SOURCE *of your prosperity.*"

HOW TO BELIEVE GOD FOR A HOUSE

by Pastor George Pearsons

from the October 2013 Believer's Voice of Victory Magazine

There's no place like home!"

My wife, Terri, and I have often declared that statement while walking through the back door of our home after a long, hard day at work. Sometimes after dinner, we will just plop down on the couch, kick up our feet and breathe a sigh of relief. I appreciate The LORD for providing the peaceful, warm atmosphere of our home. After all, He was the One who got us there in the first place!

The LORD is interested in every detail of our lives, including where we live. Our homes should be places where we can be refreshed and receive from Him. Isaiah 32:18 *(NIV)* says, "My people will live in peaceful dwelling places, in secure homes, in undisturbed places of rest."

Consider the Garden of Eden.

It was God's original intent for our earthly dwellings. The word *Eden* in the Hebrew means, "The region of Adam's home; a house of pleasure." THE BLESSING that God spoke over Adam empowered him to establish the Garden of Eden wherever he went.

That same empowerment belongs to us today.

Many do not realize that a beautiful home is part of God's wonderful plan for their lives. He is our loving, heavenly Father who knows the very desires of our hearts. He is well aware of what kind of home will minister to us. His heart is to do everything possible to fulfill that desire.

GOD'S WILL FOR YOUR HOUSE

Faith for a house begins where the will of God is known.

First John 5:14-15 *(AMP)* says:

And this is the confidence (the assurance, the privilege of boldness) which we have in Him: [we are sure] that if we ask anything (make any request) according to His will (in agreement with His own plan), He listens to and hears us. And if (since) we [positively] know that He listens to us in whatever we ask, we also know [with settled and absolute knowledge] that we have [granted us as our present possessions] the requests made of Him.

As you can see, great confidence comes when we are assured of God's will. God's Word is His perfect will and the very foundation to your house. Luke 6:48 says, "He is like a man which built an house, and digged deep, and laid the foundation on a rock: and when the flood arose, the stream beat vehemently upon that house, and could not shake it: for it was founded upon a rock."

That "rock" is God's Word.

In the course of my study, I have researched over 20 specific "house scriptures" that prove it is God's perfect will for us to live in a beautiful, debt-free home.

For instance, Proverbs 24:3-4, (AMP) says, "Through skillful and godly Wisdom is a house (a life, a home, a family) built, and by understanding it is established [on a sound and good foundation], and by knowledge shall its chambers [of every area] be filled with all precious and pleasant riches."

There it is! Your beautiful, completely furnished, debt-free house.

A DEBT-FREE STAND ON FAITH

Terri and I made a very crucial decision concerning our house.

It was the same decision Kenneth and Gloria Copeland had made many years before.

In 1967, Kenneth and Gloria determined they would immediately obey whatever they saw in God's Word. Shortly thereafter, they discovered Romans 13:8 which says, "Owe no man any thing, but to love one another."

They thought they were doomed!

"How will we ever have a car, a house or even an airplane?"

Perhaps *The Amplified Bible* would give them an "out."

On the contrary. It was even stronger.

"Keep out of debt!"

They had already dedicated themselves to The LORD, and they were determined to act on whatever He said. In spite of the seeming impossibility of ever having anything, they made their quality, uncompromising decision of no retreat, no return and no turning back. They committed to live debt free. That debt-free decision included both their personal and ministry lives.

The very first thing Gloria believed for was a house.

'I HUNG MY FAITH ON THAT SCRIPTURE'

"Satan would come to me," Gloria writes in her book, *God's Will Is Prosperity*, "with thoughts of doubt and say, 'There is no way that you can buy a house without going into debt.' When he would do that, I would trust in and continually confess 2 Corinthians 9:8 *(AMP)*. 'And God is able to make all grace (every favor and earthly blessing) come to [me] in abundance, so that [I] may always and under all circumstances and whatever the need be self-sufficient [possessing enough to require no aid or support and furnished in abundance for every good work and charitable donation].'

"It gave me the comfort and strength I needed to stand in faith," she writes. "I hung my faith on that scripture…believing God was the only way I could have my home."

They took their stand of faith, refusing to be double-minded. They meditated on the Word until their house became a reality in their hearts. They believed God's Word more than what they could see or feel, never underestimating the creative power of their faith-filled words.

They released their faith while living in Tulsa. According to Gloria, she did not realize that the construction of her first dream house in Fort Worth started the very moment she began believing God.

"Let there be a house! And there was a house."

GLORIA'S THREE REVELATIONS

It took a while before they received that house.

In the meantime, The LORD gave Gloria three revelations. This scenario fits perfectly with Proverbs 14:1 that says, "Every wise woman buildeth her house."

The first was *The Revelation of Divine Prosperity*.

The LORD showed Gloria that she could believe for divine prosperity in the same way she could believe for divine health. Both blessings already belonged to her. Jesus bore her poverty and lack in the same way He bore her sickness and disease.

We should refuse lack just as quickly as we refuse sickness.

Gloria writes, "If you make up your mind—make a quality decision—that you are not willing to live in lack, but that you are willing to live in divine prosperity and abundance, Satan cannot stop the flow of God's financial blessings."

Next was *The Revelation of Peace and Prosperity*.

Isaiah 53:5 says, "The chastisement of our peace was upon him." God tells us in Isaiah 48:17-18 *(AMP)* that He is "the Lord your God, Who teaches you to profit, Who leads you in the way that you should go. Oh, that you had hearkened to My commandments! Then your peace and prosperity would have been like a flowing river."

Peace and prosperity go hand in hand. Gloria realized that her prosperity had already been provided. It was hers now.

"By faith, we need to rest in the receiving of our homes."

The third thing The LORD showed her was *The Revelation of Dominion and Authority*. He revealed to Gloria that she had the same authority over the earth that Adam had in the Garden of Eden. Genesis 1:28 *(AMP)* says, "And God blessed them and said to them, Be fruitful, multiply, and fill the earth, and subdue it [using all its vast resources...]."

"While we were standing in faith for the money to pay for our first house, The LORD reminded me of this scripture and revealed to me that every material thing here came from the earth's vast resources—every piece of lumber, brick and glass, the concrete, and the mortar. There was nothing in the makeup of our house that had not come from the earth's resources. I had the right to take authority over it and receive it as mine in the Name of Jesus."

STAY YOUR GROUND

It took six years of standing their ground and continually acting on the Word. But the day finally came when their faith paid off. They took possession of their "beautiful, debt-free house."

As for Terri and me, our circumstances were different, but the faith principles remained the same. Here is the short version.

We owned a home, paid it off and sowed it into a family.

We then borrowed the money to buy our next house.

On a worldwide TV broadcast of the *Believer's Voice of Victory,* Brother Copeland asked me why I went back into debt. As a result, Terri and I made the quality decision to live debt free. We eventually sold the house and bought another.

The LORD worked out a way for us to purchase the new house without having to borrow the money. It took less than one year to pay off the house. And, it took four more years to renovate it by using cash. In the meantime, we lived in several rental properties.

Throughout our five years and the Copelands' six years, we all had to stand our ground. Galatians 6:9 *(AMP)* tells us to "not lose heart and grow weary and faint in acting nobly and doing right, for in due time and at the appointed season we shall reap, if we do not loosen and relax our courage and faint."

There were times when we would get discouraged, wondering if we would ever move into our house. But we determined to "not lose heart and grow weary." We continued to stand on the Word and keep our eyes focused on the desired result.

We refused to give up and quit.

We were thankful for the quality decision to pay for and renovate the house debt free. We averted a 30-year mortgage, having to pay thousands of dollars in interest, and did not have to bow our knee to a lender.

You are only one decision away from your debt-free house.

Simply make the same quality decision that Kenneth and Gloria, and Terri and I made years ago. Take your strong stand of faith in God's Word. Believe and receive Psalm 107:7 *(MSG)* that says, "He put your feet on a wonderful road that took you straight to a good place to live."

Say this out loud right now. "I speak to my house in the Name of Jesus and command it to come to me! No matter how long it takes, I am standing my ground, walking by faith and holding fast to the Word. I refuse to give up and quit. I believe I receive my beautiful, debt-free house NOW!"

Faith Scriptures
for your new home

These scriptures will produce a harvest of blessing in your home and in your life as you hold fast to your faith and do what you know to do according to the Word. God will give you a home filled with the love of God, and precious treasures."

~ GLORIA COPELAND ~

Through wisdom is an house builded; and by understanding it is established: And by knowledge shall the chambers be filled with all precious and pleasant riches.
Proverbs 24:3-4

And it shall be, when the Lord thy God shall have brought thee into the land which he swore unto thy fathers, to Abraham, to Isaac, and to Jacob, to give thee great and goodly cities, which thou buildest not, and houses full of all good things, which thou filledst not, and wells digged, which thou diggedst not, vineyards and olive trees, which thou plantedst not; when thou shalt have eaten and be full.   **Deuteronomy 6:10-11**

He led them forth by the straight and right way, that they might go to a city where they could establish their homes. Oh, that men would praise [and confess to] the Lord for His goodness and loving-kindness and His wonderful works to the children of men! For He satisfies the longing soul and fills the hungry soul with good.   **Psalm 107:7-9**, *The Amplified Bible*

Praise ye the Lord. Blessed is the man that feareth the Lord, that delighteth greatly in his commandments. His seed shall be mighty upon earth: the generation of the upright shall be blessed. Wealth and riches shall be in his house: and his righteousness endureth for ever. Unto the upright there ariseth light in the darkness: he is gracious, and full of compassion, and righteous. A good man showeth favour, and lendeth: he will guide his affairs with discretion. Surely he shall not be moved for ever: the righteous shall be in everlasting remembrance. He shall not be afraid of evil tidings: his heart is fixed, trusting in the Lord. His heart is established, he shall not be afraid, until he see his desire upon his enemies. He hath dispersed, he hath given to the poor; his righteousness endureth for ever; his horn shall be exalted with honour. The wicked shall see it, and be grieved; he shall gnash with his teeth, and melt away: the desire of the wicked shall perish.   **Psalm 112**

Prepare thy work without, and make it fit for thyself in the field; and afterwards build thine house.   **Proverbs 24:27**

In the house of the [uncompromisingly] righteous is great [priceless] treasure, but with the income of the wicked is trouble and vexation.   **Proverbs 15:6**, *The Amplified Bible*

And the effect of righteousness will be peace [internal and external], and the result of righteousness will be quietness and confident trust forever. My people shall dwell in a peaceable habitation, in safe dwellings, and in quiet resting-places.   **Isaiah 32:17-18**, *The Amplified Bible*

Thus saith the Lord of hosts, the God of Israel, unto all that are carried away captives, whom I have caused to be carried away from Jerusalem unto Babylon; Build ye houses, and dwell in them; and plant gardens, and eat the fruit of them; take ye wives, and beget sons and daughters; and take wives for your sons, and give your daughters to husbands, that they may bear sons and daughters; that ye may be increased there, and not diminished. And seek the peace of the city whither I have caused you to be carried away captives, and pray unto the Lord for it: for in the peace thereof shall ye have peace.... And Zephaniah the priest read this letter in the ears of Jeremiah the prophet.   **Jeremiah 29:4-7, 29**

Therefore they shall come and sing in the height of Zion, and shall flow together to the goodness of the Lord, for wheat, and for wine, and for oil, and for the young of the flock and of the herd: and their soul shall be as a watered garden; and they shall not sorrow any more at all. Then shall the virgin rejoice in the dance, both young men and old together: for I will turn their mourning into joy, and will comfort them, and make them rejoice from their sorrow. And I will satiate the soul of the priests with fatness, and my people shall be satisfied with my goodness, saith the Lord.   **Jeremiah 31:12-14**

Wisdom hath builded her house, she hath hewn out her seven pillars.   **Proverbs 9:1**

The blessing of the Lord, it maketh rich, and he addeth no sorrow with it.   **Proverbs 10:22**

He hushes the storm to a calm and to a gentle whisper, so that the waves of the sea are still. Then the men are glad because of the calm, and He brings them to their desired haven. Oh, that men would praise [and confess to] the Lord for His goodness and loving-kindness and His wonderful works to the children of men! Let them exalt Him also in the congregation of the people and praise Him in the company of the elders.... He turns a wilderness into a pool of water and a dry ground into water springs; and there He makes the hungry to dwell, that they may prepare a city for habitation, and sow fields, and plant vineyards which yield fruits of increase. He blesses them also, so that they are multiplied greatly, and allows not their cattle to decrease.... Yet He raises the poor and needy from affliction and makes their families like a flock. The upright shall see it and be glad, but all iniquity shall shut its mouth. Whoso is wise [if there be any truly wise] will observe and heed these things; and they will diligently consider the mercy and loving-kindness of the Lord.
Psalm 107:29-32, 35-38, 41-43,
The Amplified Bible

Thou hast caused men to ride over our heads; we went through fire and through water: but thou broughtest us out into a wealthy place.   **Psalm 66:12**

By humility and the fear of the Lord are riches, and honour, and life.   **Proverbs 22:4**

The wicked are overthrown, and are not: but the house of the righteous shall stand.
Proverbs 12:7

I called upon the Lord in distress: the Lord answered me, and set me in a large place.... This is the Lord's doing; it is marvellous in our eyes.   **Psalm 118:5, 23**

You let men ride over our heads; we went through fire and water, but you brought us to a place of abundance. **Psalm 66:12,** *New International Version*

God places the solitary in families and gives the desolate a home in which to dwell; He leads the prisoners out to prosperity; but the rebellious dwell in a parched land.... Your flock found a dwelling place in it; You, O God, in Your goodness did provide for the poor and needy.... Blessed be the Lord, Who bears our burdens and carries us day by day, even the God Who is our salvation! Selah [pause, and calmly think of that]! **Psalm 68:6,10,19,** *The Amplified Bible*

But I am poor and needy; yet the Lord thinketh upon me: thou art my help and my deliverer; make no tarrying, O my God. **Psalm 40:17**

The Spirit of the Lord is upon me, because he hath anointed me to preach the gospel to the poor; he hath sent me to heal the brokenhearted, to preach deliverance to the captives, and recovering of sight to the blind, to set at liberty them that are bruised. **Luke 4:18**

Behold, the days come, saith the Lord, that the plowman shall overtake the reaper, and the treader of grapes him that soweth seed; and the mountains shall drop sweet wine, and all the hills shall melt. And I will bring again the captivity of my people of Israel, and they shall build the waste cities, and inhabit them; and they shall plant vineyards, and drink the wine thereof; they shall also make gardens, and eat the fruit of them. And I will plant them upon their land, and they shall no more be pulled up out of their land which I have given them, saith the Lord thy God. **Amos 9:13-15**

The Lord is the portion of mine inheritance and of my cup: thou maintainest my lot. The lines are fallen unto me in pleasant places; yea, I have a goodly heritage. **Psalm 16:5-6**

Oh how great is thy goodness, which thou hast laid up for them that fear thee; which thou hast wrought for them that trust in thee before the sons of men! Thou shalt hide them in the secret of thy presence from the pride of man: thou shalt keep them secretly in a pavilion from the strife of tongues. **Psalm 31:19-20**

But we speak the wisdom of God in a mystery, even the hidden wisdom, which God ordained before the world unto our glory: Which none of the princes of this world knew: for had they known it, they would not have crucified the Lord of glory. But as it is written, Eye hath not seen, nor ear heard, neither have entered into the heart of man, the things which God hath prepared for them that love him. But God hath revealed them unto us by his Spirit: for the Spirit searcheth all things, yea, the deep things of God. **1 Corinthians 2:7-10**

And hath made of one blood all nations of men for to dwell on all the face of the earth, and hath determined the times before appointed, and the bounds of their habitation. **Acts 17:26**

Jewish commentary on Exodus 6:8
Because the Patriarchs' attitude toward this world was that they were but temporary sojourners, and that their true residence was in the heavenly world of the spirit, I promised to give them the country on earth that is most conducive to spiritual greatness.